TCHAIKOVSKY
DISCOVERS
AMERICA

Esther Kalman

ILLUSTRATED BY
Laura Fernandez and Rick Jacobson

SCHOLASTIC INC.
New York   Toronto   London   Auckland   Sydney

ISBN 0-590-64938-8

Copyright © 1994 by Classical Productions for Children Limited.
Illustrations copyright © 1994 by Laura Fernandez and Rick Jacobson.
All rights reserved. Published by Scholastic Inc., 555 Broadway, New York, NY 10012, by arrangement with Orchard Books.

12 11 10 9 8 7 6 5 4 3 2 1   6 7 8 9/9 0 1/0

Printed in the U.S.A.   14

First Scholastic printing, September 1996

Notes on Sources

Although Eugenia and her family did not exist, the details of Tchaikovsky's trip are true and are documented in his extensive diaries and letters to loved ones back in Russia.

The following books were used by the author for reference:

The Diaries of Tchaikovsky, translated from the Russian by Wladimir Lakond (New York: W. W. Norton & Company, Inc., 1945); *The Life & Letters of Peter Ilich Tchaikovsky* by Modeste Tchaikovsky, translated from the Russian by Rosa Newmarch (London: John Lane, The Bodley Head, 1906); *Piotr Ilyich Tchaikovsky: Letters to His Family: An Autobiography*, translated from the Russian by Galina Von Meck (London: Dennis Dobson, 1981); *Tchaikovsky in America: The Composer's Visit in 1891* by Elkhonon Yoffe, translated from the Russian by Lidya Yoffe (New York: Oxford University Press, 1986).

For music lovers everywhere

—E.K.

This book is dedicated to our children, Michael, Maite,
and Mercedes, with a special thank-you to Perrie,
Michael, and Peter

—L.F. & R.J.

21 May 1891

I wish I had begun this diary on May 7, my eleventh birthday, but if it had not been for what happened then, I would not be writing this now. So let me go back to my birthday and pretend I am writing in my diary every evening, to "press my memories." That is what a diary is for. I have learned that in the last two weeks.

7 May 1891

Good evening. My name is Eugenia Petroff, and I turned eleven years old today. I live in New York with Mama and Papa, my great-aunt Maria, and my brother, Alexander, who is nine. Mama, Papa, and Great-aunt Maria are Russian, but Alexander and I were born in New York. *We* are Americans: Alex and Jenny.

It has been a splendid birthday, and it is not quite over yet. The great treat is still to come. Next week Papa is going to take us to see Niagara Falls. It ought to have been this week, but a few days ago Mama asked me if I would like to go to a concert at the new Music Hall instead. She said the famous composer Peter Ilyich Tchaikovsky was conducting and there would be a matinee. Mr. Tchaikovsky's music is very special to us, and most special to me. Before I was born, Papa took Mama to see Mr. Tchaikovsky's opera *Eugene Onegin* and they decided that if their baby was a boy they would name him Eugene. The baby was me, so I was named Eugenia.

Mr. Andrew Carnegie gave the money to build the Music Hall. It is a splendid place, with sixty-two boxes and hundreds of new electric lights. The hall sits on the corner of Seventh Avenue and 57th Street, and for ages we have watched it being built. It opened two nights ago with a concert, and although Mr. Tchaikovsky was there, I am glad we were not, because as well as the music there were long, dull speeches. The newspapers said that carriages were lined up outside for a quarter mile and that Mr. Carnegie himself called Mr. Tchaikovsky the uncrowned but genuine king of music. Papa has been reading to us from the *Herald*'s reports of Mr. Tchaikovsky's visit to America.

This afternoon's concert began at two o'clock. At first Mama had her doubts about the young woman who played the piano. She hardly looked strong enough to carry the music. But when the horns sounded and she raised her hands, it seemed as if the music flowed through her fingers. Mama said the music was very Russian and she cried a little, because she was remembering Russia, perhaps. I sat very, very still while the music played, but inside I felt as though I were dancing. It was glorious!

Mama had told me Mr. Tchaikovsky was sometimes so frightened when he conducted that he could look at neither the audience nor the orchestra but would keep his eyes closed. I wanted to close my eyes, too, because the music was so sweet. Mr. Tchaikovsky had a white beard and looked rather old, but when he stood up to conduct he was like a young man again— from the back at least. I couldn't tell if his eyes were closed.

After the concert we went to a reception with hundreds of well-dressed ladies and gentlemen and a great deal of heat and noise. There was lemonade, but I had none, for fear that I would spill it on myself. Then, through the crowd, I saw Mr. Tchaikovsky, surrounded by many ladies all talking at once. Imagine going right up and speaking to him! Although he was smiling, he looked as if he did not quite understand what they were saying. I noticed that the ice cream had melted in the dish in his hands.

8 May 1891

I told my friends about the concert, but I ought to have known what they would say. Kate thought it was a dull present, although I know she was curious about Mr. Carnegie's hall. I said nothing more, for Kate's tongue is sharp, and besides, Mama says it is vulgar to boast. "Remember," she always says, "we owe our good fortune to America. If we had stayed in Russia, Papa would still be Count Petroff, but we would have no money." I know about Papa's old home in Russia. There were forty rooms, but everyone lived downstairs because the roof had fallen in.

Here in America Papa's success has come from the railroad. We will take one of his trains to Niagara Falls. We can eat breakfast and dinner in the dining car, for it takes nearly all day to get there, even on the railroad.

10 May 1891

Nothing much happened today, and I can't be bothered to try to remember any of it because I want to get on to —

This has been the most amazing day of my life! We rode in a vestibule train. We could walk up and down in it, like on a street—only the street moved as well as us. Alex and I walked up and down the train three times before we had even left New York.

Later I went for a walk on my own, and as I was passing through the dining car, I saw a gentleman sitting alone at one of the tables, writing in a book. I knew at once who it was, but I could hardly believe it. There, *in our train*, sat Mr. Tchaikovsky himself, just like an ordinary person. Just like me!

Although my hands felt icy, I was sure that even someone as famous as Mr. Tchaikovsky would not mind if a person told him how much they enjoyed his music. So I went over to the table and said, "Excuse me, sir. My name is Jenny Petroff and I wanted to tell you—"

He looked up, frowning a little when I started to speak, but then he said, "Petroff! Are you Russian?" So I started again, but this time I spoke in Russian.

I told him that my name was Eugenia Dmitrievna Petroff and that I had been to his concert. He nodded when I told him the music had made Mama so happy that she cried. How I wish Mama could have been with me to meet Mr. Tchaikovsky! She had to stay in New York with Great-aunt Maria. Someone has to stay with Auntie because she will not learn to speak English and she quarrels with the servants. If we had left her alone with them, they surely would all have quit before we got back.

Mr. Tchaikovsky said he thought I had been sent as his guardian angel, because no one on the train could understand his English. He invited me to join him for tea or coffee.

I told him I was not allowed coffee, but I would have a Coca-Cola instead. (I am not allowed that either, but I did want to try it.) The waiter said they did not serve cola, so I just ordered tea for Mr. Tchaikovsky and I asked for a saucer of jam to go with it. The waiter was surprised, but that is the Russian way, and Mr. Tchaikovsky was pleased.

I could not believe this was happening. Ever since Mr. Tchaikovsky came to New York, people have tried to see him, but here I was, just talking to him like an old friend. Slowly my icy hands seemed to thaw. Well, I couldn't just sit there telling him how marvelous he was, over and over again, so I pointed to his book and asked if he was writing music.

I thought, How wonderful if he is. I shall be the first person in the world to see it.

But he laughed and said, "No, no. This is my diary. My friends and relatives at home will want to know about America, and I have no time to write to them all, so I am putting everything into this book. When I get home, they can read it instead of letters."

I said I hoped he was telling them good things, and he said, "I am telling them amazing things! Buildings thirteen stories high, elevators that take you right to the top, hot and cold running water, the brushes, the soap, the towels—and this train! There is even a barbershop *on the train*!"

I don't know how long I had been having tea with Mr. Tchaikovsky when Alex came walking down the car looking for me. He said Papa thought I had fallen off the train.

I introduced him to Mr. Tchaikovsky. They shook hands and Mr. Tchaikovsky invited him to join us. But Alex did not understand. He hardly knows any Russian, and doesn't want to learn. He says English is good enough—but, of course, he found out at once that he was wrong about that. He wanted to talk about trains with Mr. Tchaikovsky, but they found it hard to understand each other. I had to translate.

Then Papa came along to see what had happened to Alex.

I knew he was surprised to see whom we were with, and I'm sure he was as excited as I was, but he was too much of a gentleman to show it. He bowed and asked Mr. Tchaikovsky if we were bothering him.

I don't think we were bothering Mr. Tchaikovsky. He smiled and said, "Your son has been telling me all about your railroad. Do join us."

So we all sat there and talked about trains. I was disappointed because I had wanted to tell Mr. Tchaikovsky about being named after *Eugene Onegin*.

Then, in a croaking voice that seemed to belong to someone else, I found myself asking Mr. Tchaikovsky to tell us about *Swan Lake*. Mama had seen the ballet in Moscow before she came to America and she often talked about it. But I wanted to hear the composer himself describe it.

Mr. Tchaikovsky smiled. In a whisper he said, "On the night before Prince Siegfried is to choose his bride, he and his friends go on a midnight hunt. The woods are dark and full of shadows. By the shore of an enchanted lake, Siegfried spies a magnificent, snow-white swan wearing a golden crown upon its head. He hides behind a tree and watches as the swan magically transforms itself into the most beautiful woman he has ever seen. She is Odette, the Swan Princess, and she is under the spell of the evil magician Rothbart. She and the other maidens of the court must live as swans each day from dawn until dark. Only at night can they regain their human form. To break Rothbart's curse, Siegfried must swear eternal love. But if he proves false, Odette will remain a swan forever."

Mr. Tchaikovsky did not tell me the end of the story. I suppose I shall have to wait to see the ballet. How wonderful it must be to move to Mr. Tchaikovsky's music. If only I could be a dancer, I know I would feel just like a beautiful swan.

12 May 1891

It was too late to visit the falls when we arrived last night, but we could hear them. It was so eerie to lie in the dark in a strange room and listen to the water thundering, on and on. If you did not know what was making the sound, you would never guess.

Mr. Tchaikovsky is staying at Mr. Kaltenbach's hotel, like us. At breakfast he sat at a table nearby. He was writing again, and he had a faraway look in his eyes. Papa told us not to bother him, so we just smiled, but he didn't even seem to notice us. When I walked by his table, I saw it was covered in sketches of mice and dolls. It was as if a whole toy shop were dancing across the pages of his notebook.

We took a carriage to the falls after breakfast, and Mr. Tchaikovsky was in another carriage, just in front of us. We went out to the island and looked down at the falls. The water is like green glass, and you cannot believe how fast it is moving. The best view is from the Canadian side, so we crossed over the bridge (the first time I was ever outside the United States!) and there was Mr. Tchaikovsky, just ahead of us again.

Papa said we should keep out of sight. He said it jokingly, but I believe he was serious. He was afraid Mr. Tchaikovsky might think we were newspaper reporters in disguise, following his every move, so he made us wait until Mr. Tchaikovsky had disappeared from view.

Where the river runs over the falls, it plunges straight down with a crashing roar. The sound is deafening—like an enormous orchestra performing a majestic symphony. As I stood there watching the river storm past, I looked over and saw a tiny figure on a rock below us at the foot of the falls. He was wearing a raincoat, but I recognized the white beard. It was Mr. Tchaikovsky, staring up as I was staring down, but I don't think he saw me. I wonder if he had closed his eyes.

Later, as I walked along the promenade, I heard a voice behind me. It was Mr. Tchaikovsky, but I could barely make out what he was saying through the crashing of the falls and the noise of the vendors trying to sell us picture postcards and other souvenirs. In my loudest voice I asked Mr. Tchaikovsky if he wanted to buy something to press in his diary to remind him of his trip. But he said that he had no need of mementos, that his words alone would form the memories that would be pressed between the covers. "When I read my diary back in Russia," he said, "I shall remember the sights and the sounds and the smells of America. But here in America, I am remembering Russia."

He looked so sad I thought he would cry, as Mama had done when she heard his music.

I asked him if he was homesick.

He sighed. "All the time."

We caught up with Papa and Alex, and Papa invited Mr. Tchaikovsky to share our carriage back to the hotel. Mr. Tchaikovsky went on talking about Russia to Papa, and they both sighed a great deal. Alex grew sulky and began to kick the cushions, so I translated the Russian for him. Papa said he was pining for the scent of lilac and the fields of yellow flowers. Mr. Tchaikovsky wanted to know if Papa would ever go back.

"I'm not going back," Alex growled. "It wouldn't be *back* for me. I was born in America. I'm going to stay here forever."

"You wouldn't even like to go for a visit?" asked Mr. Tchaikovsky.

I explained that Alex was afraid that, if we went for a visit, Papa would get so fond of the yellow flowers and the lilac we'd never come back again. "But we could never live in Russia now," I added, and I told him about the Petrovskova estate and the roof falling in.

Mr. Tchaikovsky laughed then and said, "Yes, that is Russia, all right. The roof is falling in. You stay here, Alexander, and build railroads."

I thought about the fields of yellow flowers and, although I have never seen them, it was as if I remembered them, too.

13 May 1891

We are staying one more night at Mr. Kaltenbach's hotel, but
Mr. Tchaikovsky left after dinner yesterday. He had to return to
New York because he was going to Baltimore next, then
Washington, then Philadelphia, and then back to New York
again—all before he could go home to Russia. Poor Mr.
Tchaikovsky, so tired and so homesick. And poor Papa. I always
thought he was being silly. I did not know that grown-ups
could get homesick.

16 May 1891

Alex tried to invent a new kind of water mill in the bathtub
and forgot to turn off the faucet. We had a flood.

18 May 1891

Mama played the piano this evening and made Alex practice the
waltz with me, for Cousin Tatiana is getting married next
month and there is to be dancing afterward. He was stepping all
over my feet—deliberately, I think.

Today I saw Mr. Tchaikovsky again. I was waiting for Papa at Central Station, and there was Mr. Tchaikovsky, going to visit some friends. We talked for a little while, and he told me he was starting his journey back to Moscow on the twenty-first.

I asked him if he would ever come back. He said he did not know and added, "I think I should be sure of a welcome if I did. I am better thought of here than I am in Russia. This is a fine country."

Then I surprised myself. I heard myself tell him, all in a rush, that I wanted to be a dancer.

In a gentle voice Mr. Tchaikovsky explained that most ballerinas begin to train at a very young age, as they do at the Maryinsky Theater in St. Petersburg. When I told him I had only just turned eleven on May 7, he laughed. "Why, that is my birthday, too. Only I have exactly forty years' start on you. We are both too old to dance at the Maryinsky, I'm afraid."

"But I dream of dancing the Swan Princess in your ballet," I confessed. I felt my face go red, because I am shy and not anything like a princess and I have such big feet.

"Perhaps you are already too old for that," he said very kindly. "But you must never stop loving the ballet. You do not have to dance in a great theater to be a dancer. It is a matter of the heart."

I knew he understood how much I love to dance. Although his train was waiting, he told me a story of when he was a boy. One night after a party his governess found him frightened and upset in his bed. "Oh, this music, this music! Take it away!" he had cried, holding his head. "It's in here and it won't let me sleep!"

"It has always been this way," he explained to me. "Music will never leave me alone."

We heard Mr. Tchaikovsky's train blow its last whistle. "Well, now we must part, Eugenia Dmitrievna — or should I call you Miss Jenny?"

"Either," I said. "Both. I'm American, like Alex, but I am Russian, too."

"Then good-bye, Miss Jenny," he said. "Let us remember each other in friendship."

And he went away.

20 May 1891

Uncle Fyodor, in Chicago, sent me some money for my birthday. I was saving it until I saw something I really wanted, and today I did. It is a beautiful book with leather binding and marbled edges and five hundred blank pages. It has no words in it until I put them there.

The book is my diary, and this is where it truly begins.

     Today Peter Ilyich Tchaikovsky, my friend, sails away from New York back to Russia.

     He is the first person I have written about in my diary. I wonder if he has put me in his.